How to Prepare for a Hurricane

A Complete Guide to Preparing for and Surviving the Storm

Noah Deschamps

<u>Table of Contents:</u>

Introduction

Hurricanes, nature's relentless juggernauts, possess the formidable ability to wreak havoc on coastal communities, causing widespread devastation in their path. These ferocious storms leave little room for error, making preparedness an absolute necessity.

Welcome to "How to Prepare for a Hurricane." In the pages that follow, we will embark on a journey to equip you with the essential knowledge and skills required to navigate the complex terrain of hurricane preparedness.

This guide will delve into the science behind hurricanes, offering insights into their formation and the factors that influence their strength. We'll help you assess your personal risk and identify your local evacuation zones, empowering you to create a well-informed and effective hurricane preparedness plan.

Securing your home is paramount, and we will explore practical strategies for safeguarding your residence, from reinforcing its structural integrity to fortifying windows and doors. Furthermore, we'll emphasize the importance of assembling a hurricane preparedness kit and establishing a family emergency communication plan.

When evacuation becomes necessary, we will provide guidance on when and how to leave, as well as tips for finding suitable shelters and accommodations. Surviving the hurricane itself is a daunting task, and we'll share valuable insights on staying safe during the storm's fury.

As the storm passes and the recovery process begins, we will address the challenges of dealing with power outages, water shortages, and the steps required to return home and rebuild your life.

By the time you reach the final chapter of this guide, you will be armed with the knowledge and confidence needed to confront a hurricane head-on, secure in the knowledge that you have taken the necessary steps to protect yourself, your loved ones, and your property.

So, let us embark on this journey together, as we demystify the world of hurricanes and empower you not only to withstand the storm but to emerge from it stronger and more resilient.

Chapter 1: Understanding Hurricanes

Hurricanes are some of the most powerful and destructive natural phenomena on Earth. These immense storms, also known as cyclones or typhoons in different parts of the world, are capable of causing widespread devastation. To prepare effectively for a hurricane, it's essential to first understand what these storms are and how they work.

1.1 What Is a Hurricane?

A hurricane is a massive, rotating storm that forms over warm ocean waters. It is characterized by strong winds, heavy rainfall, and, in some cases, storm surges. Hurricanes can vary in size and intensity, but they all share common features that make them unique.

1.2 The Birth of a Hurricane

Hurricanes start as tropical disturbances over warm ocean waters. When certain conditions are met, these disturbances can evolve into tropical depressions and eventually develop into hurricanes. Warm sea surface temperatures, moist air, and relatively low wind shear are all factors that contribute to hurricane formation.

1.3 Hurricane Classification

Hurricanes are classified based on their wind speed and intensity using the Saffir-Simpson Hurricane Wind Scale. The scale ranges from Category 1 (weakest) to Category 5 (strongest). Each category has specific wind speed thresholds, and these classifications help meteorologists and the public understand the potential impact of an approaching storm.

1.4 Anatomy of a Hurricane

Understanding the structure of a hurricane is crucial for preparedness. A hurricane consists of several key components:

- **Eye**: The calm center of the hurricane where skies are clear.
- **Eyewall**: The ring of intense thunderstorms surrounding the eye with the strongest winds and heaviest rainfall.
- **Rainbands**: Bands of clouds and rain that spiral outward from the eyewall.

1.5 The Life Cycle of a Hurricane

Hurricanes go through a life cycle that includes formation, growth, maturity, and decay. Tracking this life cycle helps forecasters predict a hurricane's path and intensity. Factors such as sea surface temperatures, atmospheric conditions, and the presence of other weather systems can influence a hurricane's behavior.

1.6 Historical Hurricanes

Throughout history, there have been memorable hurricanes that have left a lasting impact on communities and regions. Studying these historical hurricanes can provide valuable insights into the destructive potential of these storms and the importance of preparedness. Additionally, with the changing climate, understanding how hurricanes may evolve in the future is crucial for planning and mitigation efforts.

In this chapter, we've laid the foundation for a deeper understanding of hurricanes. Armed with this knowledge, you'll be better equipped to make informed decisions as we delve into the practical aspects of hurricane preparedness in the following chapters.

Chapter 2: Creating a Hurricane Preparedness Plan

When it comes to facing a hurricane, having a well-thought-out plan can make all the difference in ensuring the safety of yourself and your loved ones. In this chapter, we will guide you through the process of creating a comprehensive hurricane preparedness plan that covers all aspects of readiness.

2.1 Assessing Your Risk and Local Evacuation Zones

Before you can prepare effectively for a hurricane, it's crucial to understand your level of risk and the specific challenges your location may face. We will discuss:

- Identifying your geographical vulnerability
- Understanding hurricane-related hazards
- Determining your local evacuation zones

2.2 Assembling a Hurricane Preparedness Kit

A well-stocked hurricane preparedness kit is a cornerstone of your readiness plan. We will cover:

- Essential supplies to include in your kit
- Special considerations for medical needs and pets

- Maintaining and replenishing your kit

2.3 Developing a Family Emergency Communication Plan

In times of crisis, communication is paramount. Creating a family emergency communication plan is vital. Topics will include:

- Establishing a central point of contact
- Communication methods and backups
- Sharing important information with family members and loved ones

2.4 Understanding the Importance of Insurance

Insurance can be a lifeline after a hurricane. We will explore:

- Types of insurance coverage to consider
- The claims process and documentation
- Mitigating risk through insurance

2.5 Planning for Special Needs and Vulnerable Populations

Hurricane preparedness should consider the unique needs of all family members and community members. We will discuss:

- Preparing for individuals with disabilities

- Assisting elderly family members and neighbors
- Ensuring the safety of children and infants

A well-crafted hurricane preparedness plan is your roadmap to safety and security when a hurricane threatens. By the end of this chapter, you'll be well on your way to developing a plan tailored to your specific circumstances, ensuring that you and your loved ones are ready for the challenges that may lie ahead.

Chapter 3: Securing Your Home

Your home is your sanctuary, and during a hurricane, it's essential to take steps to protect it from the devastating forces of the storm. In this chapter, we will explore the measures you can take to secure your residence and increase your chances of weathering the hurricane safely.

3.1 Reinforcing Your Home's Structural Integrity

A sturdy home is better equipped to withstand hurricane-force winds. We will cover:

- Inspecting your home's structural integrity
- Strengthening roof and wall connections
- Retrofitting your home for hurricane resistance

3.2 Protecting Windows and Doors

Windows and doors are vulnerable points during a hurricane. We will discuss:

- Installing hurricane shutters and impact-resistant glass
- Reinforcing garage doors
- Securing sliding glass doors and double-entry doors

3.3 Securing Outdoor Objects and Trimming Trees

Flying debris can pose a significant threat during a hurricane. We will explore:

- Securing outdoor furniture and objects
- Trimming trees and shrubs to reduce hazards
- Clearing debris from gutters and drains

3.4 Ensuring Access to Clean Water and Backup Power

Maintaining access to clean water and backup power is essential. Topics will include:

- Storing an ample supply of drinking water
- Backup power options, including generators and solar panels
- Safely operating generators during power outages

3.5 Creating a Safe Room

In extreme situations, having a designated safe room can be a lifesaver. We will cover:

- Selecting an appropriate location for a safe room
- Constructing a safe room or fortifying an existing space
- Equipping your safe room with essentials

By taking these steps to secure your home, you'll greatly increase your chances of protecting your property and the well-being of your family during a hurricane. As you read through this chapter, consider how these measures can be applied to your specific situation and make plans to implement them as part of your hurricane preparedness strategy.

Chapter 4: Evacuation and Shelter Options

In some cases, the safest course of action during a hurricane is to evacuate your home and seek shelter in a designated safe location. This chapter will guide you through the crucial decisions and preparations needed to evacuate effectively and find appropriate shelter.

4.1 When and How to Evacuate

Timing and readiness are key when it comes to evacuating before a hurricane. We will discuss:

- Recognizing evacuation orders and warnings
- Planning your evacuation route
- Preparing your vehicle for evacuation

4.2 Finding Suitable Shelters and Accommodations

Knowing where to go for shelter is vital. Topics will include:

- Identifying local emergency shelters
- Shelter options for pets and livestock
- Considerations for staying with friends or family

4.3 What to Bring When Evacuating

Packing essential supplies and documents is essential when evacuating. We will cover:

- Assembling an emergency evacuation kit
- Important documents to bring
- Preserving sentimental and valuable items

4.4 Staying Informed During Evacuation

Staying informed about the hurricane's progress is critical while on the move. We will explore:

- Reliable sources of information
- Keeping communication lines open
- Making informed decisions during your evacuation journey

During a hurricane, your safety and that of your loved ones take precedence. This chapter will help you understand the importance of evacuation when necessary and guide you through the process of finding suitable shelter and preparing for the journey. As you read through this chapter, consider how these guidelines can be applied to your specific circumstances to ensure a safe evacuation.

Chapter 5: Surviving and Recovering After the Hurricane

Surviving the immediate impact of a hurricane is only the beginning. After the storm passes, a new set of challenges emerges. This chapter is dedicated to the actions and strategies you should take to ensure your safety and recovery in the aftermath of a hurricane.

5.1 Staying Safe During the Storm

Even after the hurricane has made landfall, dangers persist. We will discuss:

- Safety precautions during the storm
- Avoiding downed power lines and standing water
- How to handle emergencies during the hurricane

5.2 Dealing with Power Outages and Water Shortages

Loss of power and access to clean water are common post-hurricane issues. Topics will include:

- Preparing for extended power outages
- Safe use of generators and alternative energy sources

- Purifying water for drinking and sanitation

5.3 After the Storm: Returning Home Safely

Returning home requires careful planning to ensure your safety. We will explore:

- Assessing damage and potential hazards
- Securing your property and belongings
- The importance of patience and caution

5.4 Coping with the Aftermath and Rebuilding

Recovery after a hurricane can be a long and challenging process. We will cover:

- Emotional and psychological recovery
- Navigating insurance claims and assistance programs
- Rebuilding your home and community

5.5 Community Resilience and Preparedness for Future Hurricanes

Hurricanes often bring communities together. We will discuss:

- The role of neighbors and community support
- How to participate in disaster preparedness efforts
- Learning from the hurricane experience

As you read through this chapter, consider how these strategies and recommendations can help you not only survive the immediate aftermath of a hurricane but also rebuild and recover. Your resilience and preparedness will play a crucial role in the journey toward normalcy and the ongoing safety of your community.

Conclusion

In the face of nature's fiercest adversary, a hurricane, your preparedness and knowledge are your greatest assets. Throughout this book, "How to Prepare for a Hurricane," we have embarked on a comprehensive journey to equip you with the essential tools and strategies needed to face the challenges posed by these formidable storms.

From understanding the intricate science behind hurricanes to creating a thorough hurricane preparedness plan, securing your home, making informed decisions about evacuation, and surviving and recovering in the aftermath, you've been provided with a wealth of knowledge and actionable steps to protect yourself, your loved ones, and your property.

As you close this book, remember that preparedness is an ongoing process. Regularly review and update your plans and supplies, stay informed about local evacuation routes and shelter options, and actively participate in your community's disaster preparedness efforts.

Hurricanes may be relentless, but your resilience and readiness can help you weather the storm and emerge stronger on the other side. By taking the steps outlined in this guide and remaining vigilant in the face of hurricane threats, you have taken a proactive stance in ensuring your safety and the well-being of your community.

Thank you for entrusting us to guide you through the world of hurricane preparedness. Remember, you are not alone in this journey. Together, we can face the tempests of nature and emerge as survivors, ready to rebuild and thrive once more.

Stay safe, stay prepared, and may you always find strength in knowledge and resilience in readiness.

Appendix 1: Hurricane Preparedness Checklist

Before the Storm:

- Evaluate your risk based on your location.
- Identify your local evacuation zones.
- Subscribe to weather alerts and monitor forecasts regularly.
- Create a family emergency communication plan.
- Gather important documents (identification, insurance, property titles).
- Assemble a comprehensive first aid kit.
- Prepare an emergency kit with non-perishable food, water, flashlights, batteries, and basic tools.
- Store enough clean drinking water for at least three days.
- Arrange for pet supplies if you have pets.
- Ensure your cellphone is charged and have an external battery on hand.
- Secure windows with shutters or X-shaped tape if necessary.

During Evacuation:

- Follow official evacuation orders.
- Inform someone of your destination and route.
- Take clothing, bedding, medications, and valuables with you.
- Bring your emergency and first aid kits.
- Evacuate promptly and avoid driving through flooded areas.

During the Storm:

- Stay indoors and away from windows.
- Listen to the radio or weather alerts for updates.
- Avoid using candles during power outages; use battery-powered flashlights.
- Keep your cellphone charged and use it sparingly.
- Be prepared to seek shelter in a safe location if necessary.

After the Storm:

- Wait for official announcements that the alert is over.
- Avoid flooded areas and fallen power lines.

- Inspect your home for damage and ensure it's safe to return.
- Report any damage to your insurance company.
- Assist neighbors in need and collaborate with the community for repair and recovery efforts.

Appendix 2:Emergency Kit Inventory List

Preparing an emergency kit is a crucial part of hurricane preparedness. This checklist will help you ensure that your emergency kit is well-stocked and ready to use when needed. Review and update your kit regularly to ensure its contents remain fresh and functional.

Food and Water Supplies

- Non-perishable food items (canned goods, dried fruits, granola bars)
- Manual can opener
- At least one gallon of water per person per day for at least three days
- Water purification tablets or a portable water filter

First Aid and Medical Supplies

- First aid kit with bandages, antiseptic wipes, and adhesive tape
- Prescription medications (if applicable) with a copy of prescriptions

- Over-the-counter medications (pain relievers, antacids, etc.)
- Medical supplies (gloves, scissors, tweezers, thermometer)
- Personal hygiene items (toothbrush, toothpaste, soap, hand sanitizer)

Tools and Supplies

- Battery-powered or hand-crank radio
- Flashlights with extra batteries
- Multi-tool or utility knife
- Whistle
- Duct tape
- Plastic sheeting and garbage bags for shelter and sanitation

Clothing and Bedding

- Change of clothing for each family member
- Sturdy shoes or boots
- Warm blankets or sleeping bags
- Rain ponchos or waterproof jackets

Personal Documents and Essentials

- Important documents (identification, insurance policies, medical records)
- Cash (small bills and coins)
- Cellphone with a portable charger or solar charger
- Family emergency plan and contact information
- Maps of your local area and evacuation routes

Miscellaneous Items

- Childcare supplies (if applicable, such as diapers and formula)
- Pet supplies (if applicable, including food, water, leash, and carriers)
- Entertainment (books, games, and activities to pass the time)
- Notepad and pen

Remember to personalize your emergency kit to meet the specific needs of your family, taking into consideration the number of family members, any special medical or dietary requirements, and the local climate. Regularly check the expiration dates of food and medications, replace batteries, and update documents to ensure your kit remains current and effective.

Having a well-prepared emergency kit is a key component of hurricane readiness, providing you with essential supplies during the critical hours and days following a hurricane's impact.